Learning Math

Grade 1

This book has been designed to help children learn important math skills and some fascinating aspects of God's teachings at the same time. It addresses important fundamental first grade math skills (memorization of facts, math procedures, etc.) and also stresses the importance of understanding the basic concepts involved in math.

Learning Math With Noah provides children with practice in concept development (understanding the process) and provides opportunities for skill practice as well. All activities are presented in an interesting format that is child-friendly.

As you might expect from looking at the title of this book, each activity presented features some aspect of God's teachings. Use these lessons as building blocks for further discussions. This book is a wonderful way to help children learn math concepts and skills using a religious format. It will also help children see math as an important part of their everyday lives.

How to Use This Book

- Provide a quiet, comfortable place in which you can work with the child.
- Create a warm, accepting atmosphere so that the child will feel successful.
- Make sure that the child understands the directions before beginning an activity. This may require you reading material presented on each page to him or her.
- Offer praise and encouragement to the child throughout each activity.
- Check the answers with the child as soon as an activity has been completed. (Answers are provided on the pull-out pages in the center of the book.)
- Math topics included in this book are as follows: counting, skip counting, writing numbers, adding, subtracting, comparing numbers, sorting, patterning, identifying even and odd numbers, graphing, measuring, telling time, identifying equal parts, naming coins and their values, and much more.
- Cut out the manipulatives on pages 51-52. Have the child color them. Store the pieces in a sealable plastic bag. On page C of the pull-out pages are helpful suggestions for using the manipulatives.
- Reward the child for his or her hard work with the award on page D of the pull-out pages. This is a great way to boost a child's self-esteem!

Counting With Noah

Noah was a good man. He had a pure heart and loved God. God loved Noah, too.

Look at God's creations below. Trace the numbers. Then write the numbers on the lines.

1 2 3 4

5 6 7 8

   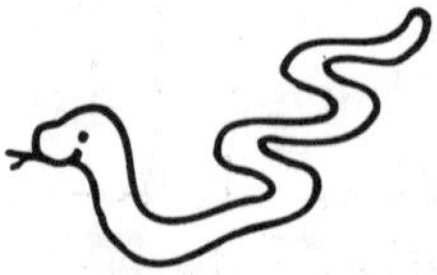

9 10 11 12

 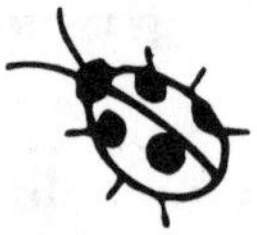  

13 14 15 16

Noah Obeyed God

God told Noah to build an ark. Noah was a faithful man who obeyed God. He built the ark.

Look at the picture. Write the numbers 1-10 in the boxes.

Find the Missing Animals

God told Noah to bring two of every living thing into the ark and protect them from the flood.

Fill in the missing numbers.

1		3	4		6	7	8		10
11	12	13		15	16		18	19	
21	22		24		26	27		29	30
	32	33	34	35		37		39	40
41	42		44	45	46		48	49	
51		53	54		56	57		59	60
61		63	64	65	66		68		70
	72	73		75		77	78	79	80
81	82	83		85	86	87		89	
	92	93	94		96	97	98		100

Noah Saved Many Animals

Noah obeyed God and found two of every living thing. Noah gathered food for the animals, too.

Write the numbers 1 to 100 below.

1	2	3							

Two by Two

The animals came into the ark two by two.

Practice counting by twos. Trace the numbers of the animals entering the ark. Then write the numbers.

2 2

10

8

4

6

And More Animals Came

Two…four…six…eight…the animals kept coming into the ark.

Count by twos. Write the numbers on the lines.

The Birds Came

Noah saved the birds! Two of every kind of bird joined Noah in the ark.

Count by fives to connect the dots. You will find two of the birds Noah saved.

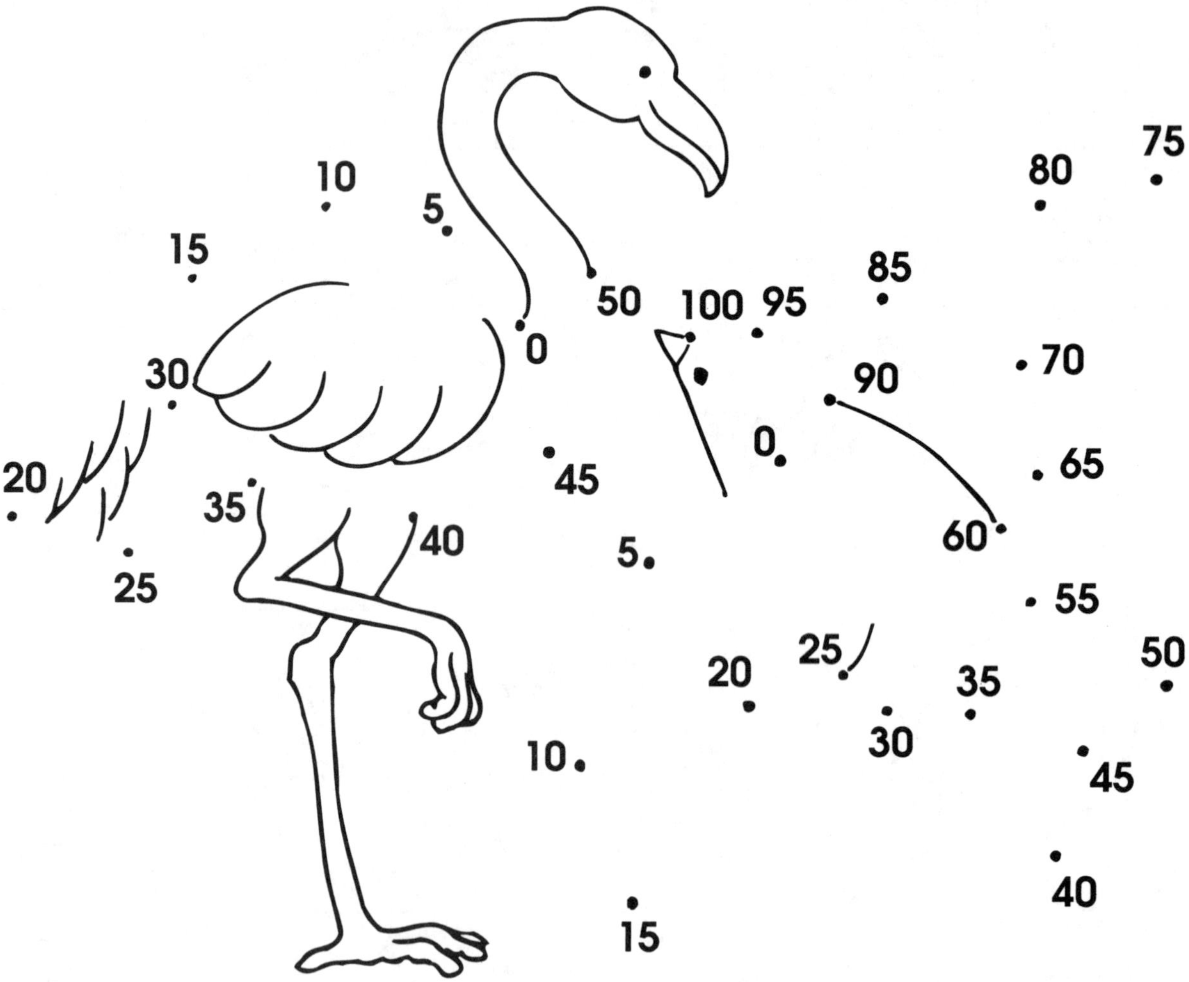

The Monkeys Came

Noah saved the monkeys!

Find the monkey and its food in the picture. Count by fives to connect the dots.

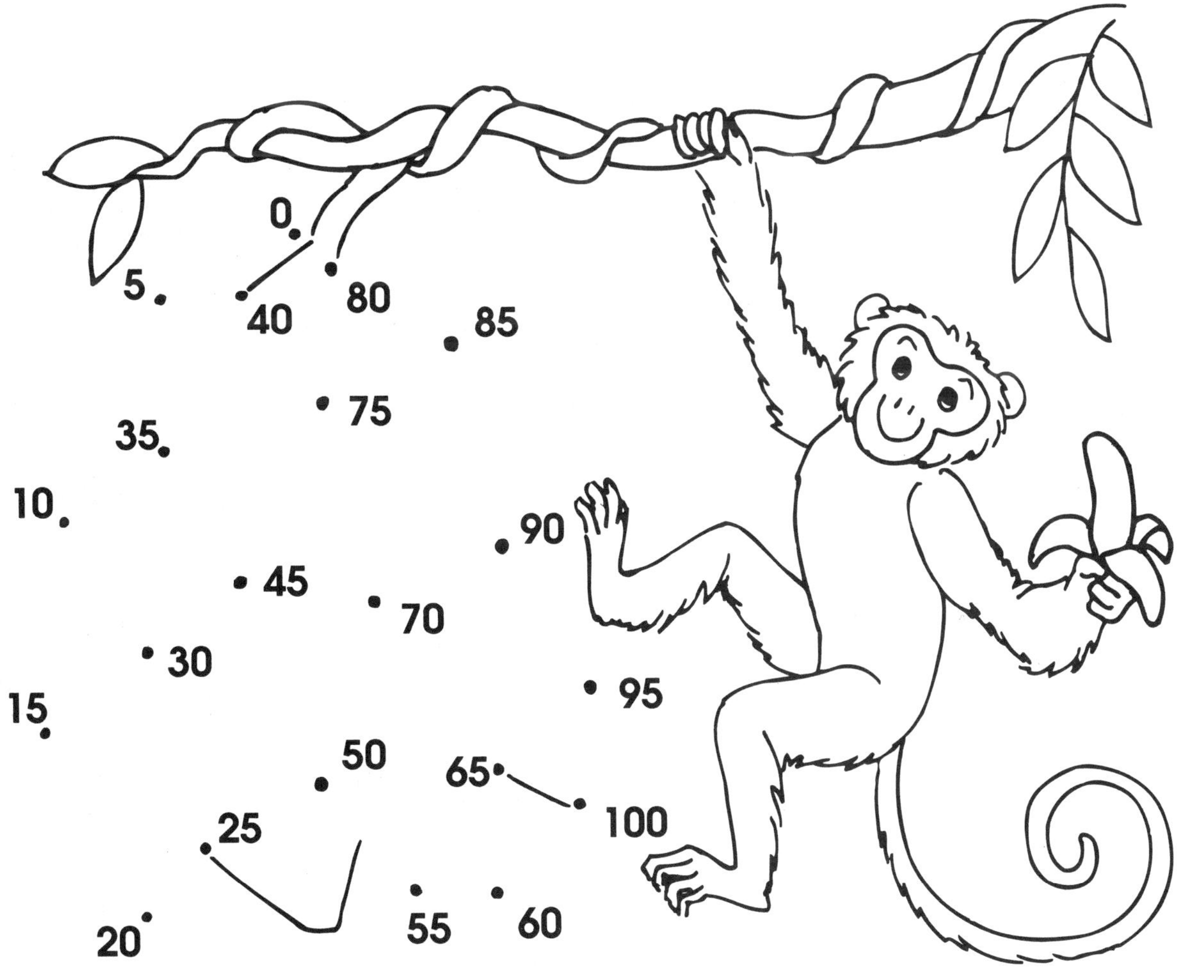

The Lions Came

Noah saved the lions! Imagine the lions' loud roar in the ark.

Count by tens to connect the dots. Pretend you hear the lion roar.

Insects Were Invited, Too!

Every creepy, crawling thing joined Noah in the ark.

Look at the groups of insects. Write an addition sentence.

A.

________ + ________ = ________

B.

________ + ________ = ________

C.

________ + ________ = ________

D.

________ + ________ = ________

The Rain Came Down

God gave Noah seven days to gather the animals. Then God sent the rain to the earth. God promised to keep Noah, his family, and the animals safe on the ark.

Look at the big and small raindrops. Write your own addition story about the raindrops.

Covered by Love

God loved and protected Noah and the animals in the ark. God loves and protects us too.

Find the sums.

$3 + 4 = $ ____

$2 + 9 = $ ____

$3 + 6 = $ ____

$5 + 4 = $ ____

$6 + 6 = $ ____

$7 + 3 = $ ____

$8 + 4 = $ ____

$6 + 5 = $ ____

They All Add Up!

The animals lived in peace in the ark.

Write an addition sentence.

A.

_____ + _____ = _____

B.

_____ + _____ = _____

C.

_____ + _____ = _____

D.

_____ + _____ = _____

E.

_____ + _____ = _____

F.

_____ + _____ = _____

The Water Rises

Each day, the water rose. The ark was lifted above the earth, floating on the water. Even the high mountains under the heavens were slowly covered.

Find the differences.

Addition of 2-digit and 1-digit numbers

Noah's Numbers

There are lots of numbers in the story of Noah and the flood. For example, it took a certain number of days to build the ark. Also, it rained for 40 days and nights. Even Noah's age was a number.

Find the sums.

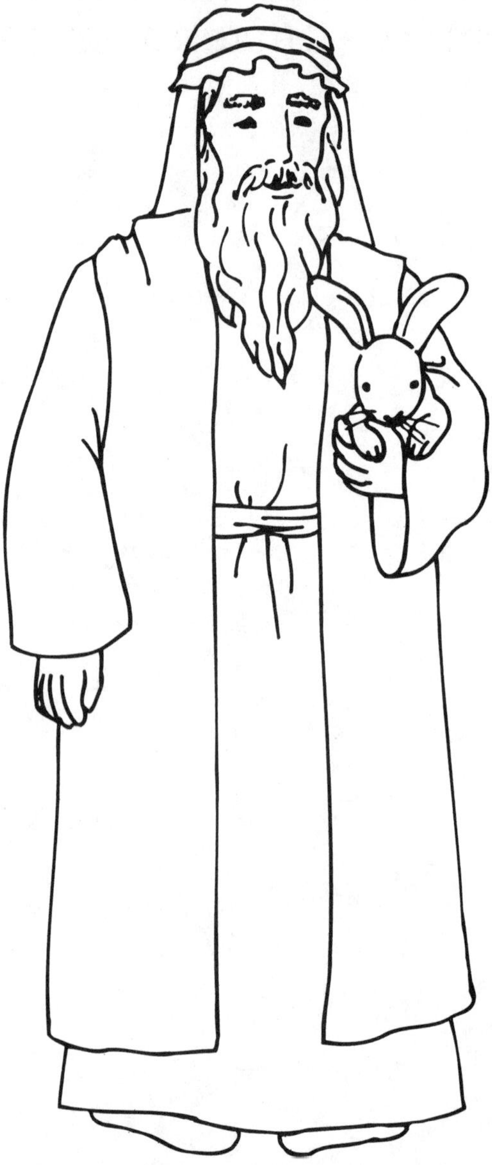

12 + 3	10 + 6	15 + 3
18 + 2	11 + 8	13 + 3
16 + 2	7 + 12	8 + 10
14 + 7	17 + 2	19 + 1

Where Is the Sun?

For 40 days, clouds filled the sky sending more and more rain on earth.

Look at the clouds. Write a subtraction sentence.

	Raindrops in All		Number of Raindrops That Fell		Number of Raindrops Left
A.	 ______	–	 ______	=	 ______
B.	 ______	–	 ______	=	 ______
C.	 ______	–	 ______	=	 ______
D.	 ______	–	 ______	=	 ______

Twice as Nice

God didn't want Noah to bring just one of each animal on the ark. He wanted two of each animal!

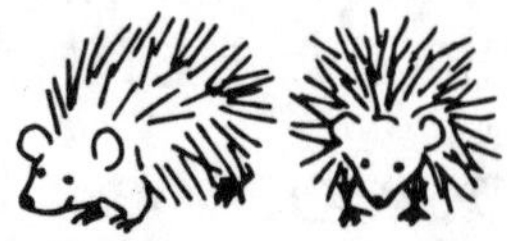

Write the sum for each doubles fact.

A.					
4	5	6	7	8	9
+ 4	+ 5	+ 6	+ 7	+ 8	+ 9

Use the doubles facts to find sums for those doubles.

B.				
4	5	6	5	4
+ 5	+ 6	+ 7	+ 4	+ 3

4 + 4 = 8 so 4 + 5 must be 1 more = 9

C.					
8	7	6	3	7	9
+ 9	+ 8	+ 5	+ 4	+ 6	+ 8

Write near doubles for the doubles fact. Write the sum.

D. 2 + 2 = ____
____ + ____ = ____
____ + ____ = ____

E. 4 + 4 = ____
____ + ____ = ____
____ + ____ = ____

F. 6 + 6 = ____
____ + ____ = ____
____ + ____ = ____

G. 7 + 7 = ____
____ + ____ = ____
____ + ____ = ____

H. 9 + 9 = ____
____ + ____ = ____
____ + ____ = ____

Day and Night

Day and night, Noah cared for the animals. Noah fed the animals on the ark.

Subtract the number of  each elephant eats.

A.
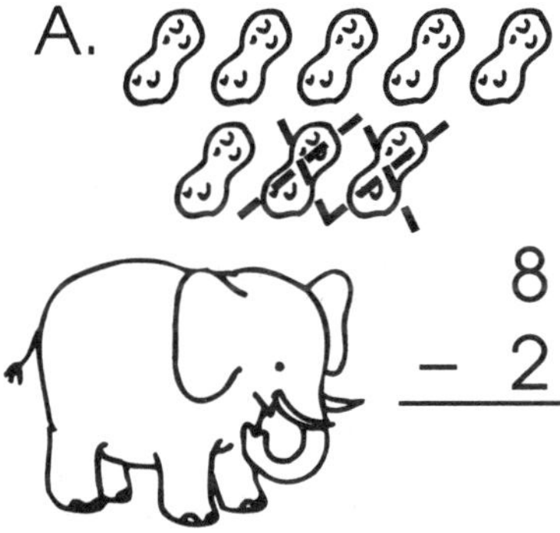

$$\begin{array}{r} 8 \\ -\ 2 \\ \hline \end{array}$$

B.
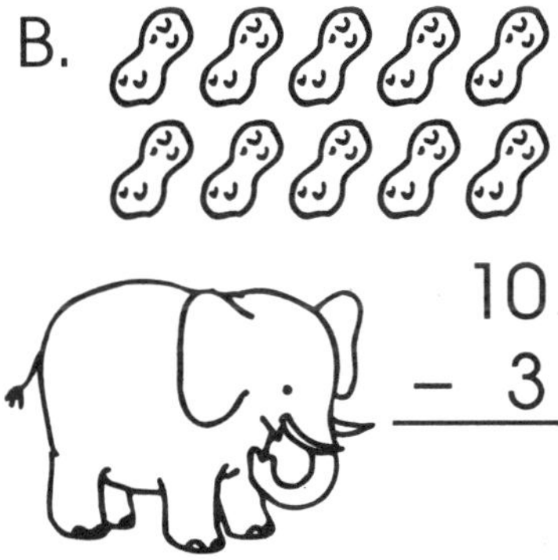

$$\begin{array}{r} 10 \\ -\ 3 \\ \hline \end{array}$$

C.

$$\begin{array}{r} 6 \\ -\ 2 \\ \hline \end{array}$$

D.

$$\begin{array}{r} 7 \\ -\ 4 \\ \hline \end{array}$$

E.

$$\begin{array}{r} 5 \\ -\ 1 \\ \hline \end{array}$$

F.

$$\begin{array}{r} 9 \\ -\ 5 \\ \hline \end{array}$$

G.

$$\begin{array}{r} 9 \\ -\ 3 \\ \hline \end{array}$$

H.

$$\begin{array}{r} 8 \\ -\ 6 \\ \hline \end{array}$$

I.

$$\begin{array}{r} 10 \\ -\ 5 \\ \hline \end{array}$$

Big and Small Raindrops

Big and small raindrops fell while Noah was in the ark.
Write a subtraction sentence.

A. 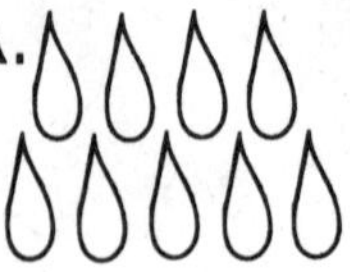

_____ – _____ = _____

B. 

_____ – _____ = _____

C. 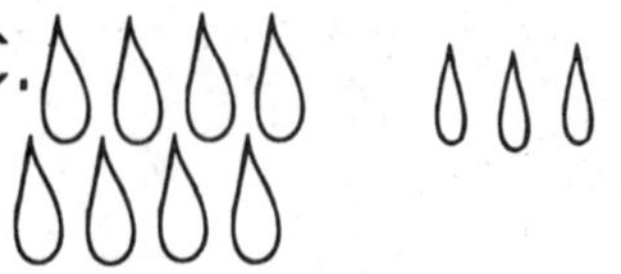

_____ – _____ = _____

D. 

_____ – _____ = _____

E. 

_____ – _____ = _____

F. 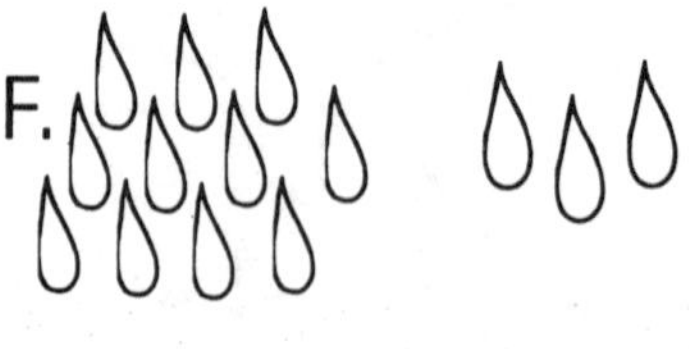

_____ – _____ = _____

G. 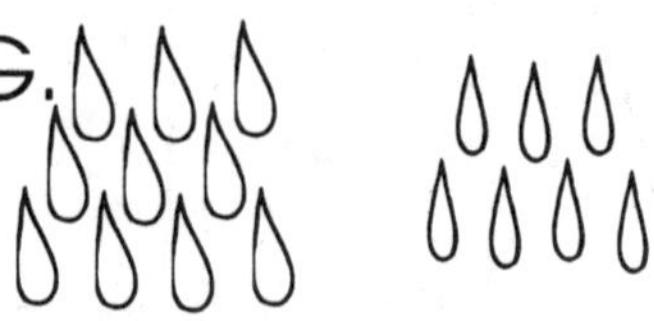

_____ – _____ = _____

H. 

_____ – _____ = _____

Great Giraffe

Noah's ark was 45 feet high. This is as high as a five-story building. It was even tall enough for a giraffe that is about 18 feet tall.

Find the differences.

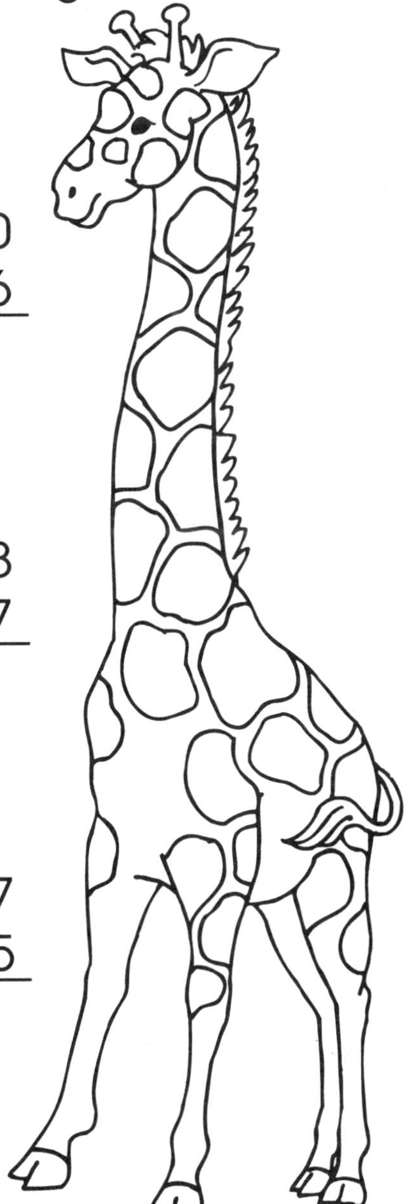

A. $\begin{array}{r} 18 \\ -\ 8 \\ \hline \end{array}$ $\begin{array}{r} 17 \\ -\ 3 \\ \hline \end{array}$ $\begin{array}{r} 10 \\ -\ 6 \\ \hline \end{array}$

B. $\begin{array}{r} 16 \\ -\ 4 \\ \hline \end{array}$ $\begin{array}{r} 12 \\ -\ 8 \\ \hline \end{array}$ $\begin{array}{r} 18 \\ -\ 7 \\ \hline \end{array}$

C. $\begin{array}{r} 13 \\ -\ 7 \\ \hline \end{array}$ $\begin{array}{r} 15 \\ -\ 8 \\ \hline \end{array}$ $\begin{array}{r} 17 \\ -\ 5 \\ \hline \end{array}$

Back to Noah

When the rain stopped, Noah sent out a dove to find dry land. The dove didn't find any and came back.

Add or subtract.

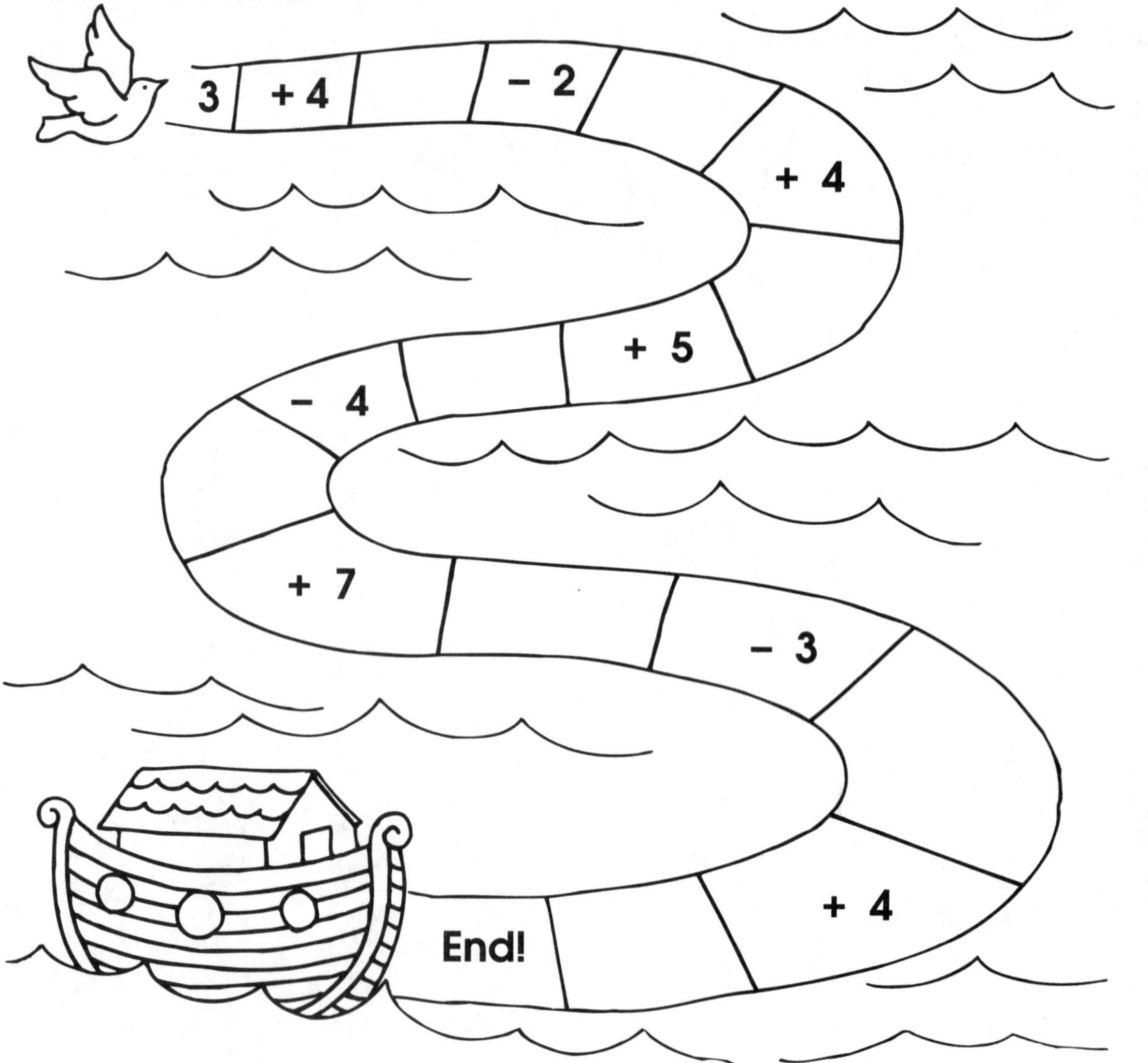

Creatures Large and Small

Noah made the ark big enough for large and small creatures.

Look at the numbers on each pair of animals. Color the animals with the larger number.

Color the animals with the smaller number.

Room for All

There was room for Noah and the animals on the ark.

Use > and < to compare the numbers.

Animals Move Around

Noah and the animals moved around the ark.

Look at the animals below. Color the animals that crawl blue. Color the animals that walk red. Color the animals that fly purple.

Pretty Peacocks

Imagine all the beautiful colors the animals brought to the ark.

Peacocks have beautiful feathers. Continue the patterns.

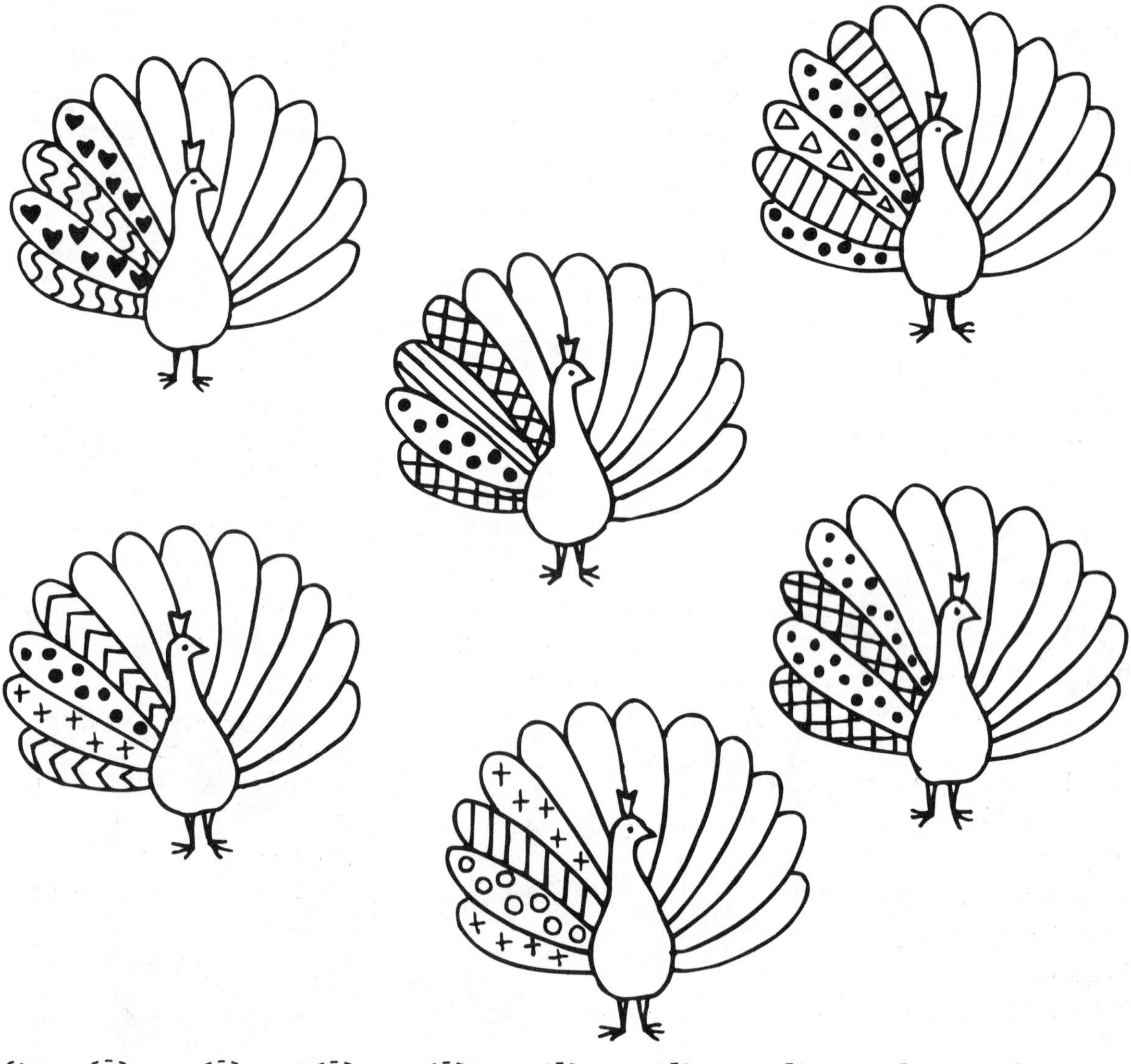

Pull-Out Answers

Page 3

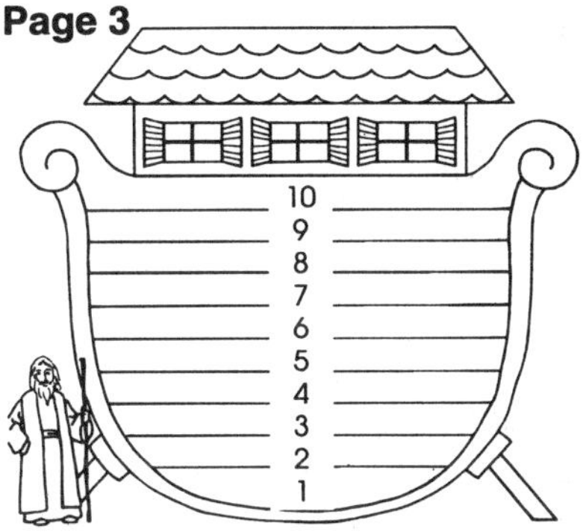

Pages 4-5

1	2	3	4	5	6	7	8	9	10
11	12	13	14	15	16	17	18	19	20
21	22	23	24	25	26	27	28	29	30
31	32	33	34	35	36	37	38	39	40
41	42	43	44	45	46	47	48	49	50
51	52	53	54	55	56	57	58	59	60
61	62	63	64	65	66	67	68	69	70
71	72	73	74	75	76	77	78	79	80
81	82	83	84	85	86	87	88	89	90
91	92	93	94	95	96	97	98	99	100

Page 6

2, 4, 6, 8, 10

Page 7

12, 14, 16, 18, 20, 22, 24, 26, 28, 30

Page 11

A. 2 + 3 = 5
B. 1 + 4 = 5
C. 4 + 4 = 8
D. 3 + 4 = 7

Page 12

Stories may vary. There are 10 raindrops in all.

Page 13

7, 11, 9, 12, 10, 9, 12, 11

Page 14

A. 4 + 2 = 6
B. 8 + 3 = 11
C. 3 + 9 = 12
D. 2 + 5 = 7
E. 3 + 6 = 9
F. 7 + 5 = 12

Page 15

4, 5, 3, 2, 3, 2, 1, 2

Page 16

15, 16, 18; 20, 19, 16;
18, 19, 18; 21, 19, 20

Page 17

A. 4 – 2 = 2
B. 6 – 4 = 2
C. 5 – 4 = 1
D. 8 – 3 = 5

Page 18

A. 8, 10, 12, 14, 16, 18
B. 9, 11, 13, 9, 7
C. 17, 15, 11, 7, 13, 17
D. 4, 3 + 2 = 5, 2 + 1 = 3
E. 8, 4 + 5 = 9, 3 + 4 = 7
F. 12, 6 + 7 = 13, 6 + 5 = 11
G. 14, 8 + 7 = 15, 7 + 6 = 13
H. 18, 10 + 9 = 19, 8 + 9 = 17

Page 19

A. 6 B. 7 C. 4
D. 3 E. 4 F. 4
G. 6 H. 2 I. 5

Page 20

A. 9 – 2 = 7
B. 10 – 4 = 6
C. 8 – 3 = 5
D. 12 – 4 = 8
E. 9 – 6 = 3
F. 11 – 3 = 8
G. 10 – 7 = 3
H. 12 – 5 = 7

Page 21

A. 10, 14, 4
B. 12, 4, 11
C. 6, 7, 12

Page 22

Page 23

elephant, duck, ostrich, frog; camel, lizard, cow, fox

Page 24

<, <; <, >; <, >

Page 25

blue: snake, worm; red: cow, giraffe, horse, monkey, squirrel; purple: bird, butterfly, owl, parrot

Page 26

Children should continue the patterns.

Page 27

even: 10, 42, 2, 16, 4, 20, 32, 58, 6, 8, 46, 18, 84, 36, 64; odd: 19, 31, 17, 13, 5, 9, 65, 3, 87, 53, 93, 71, 55, 37, 7

Page 28

odd: 21, 17, 33, 25, 81, 3, 29, 47, 7, 5, 9, 39, 15, 73, 51; even: 10, 22, 34, 32, 46, 2, 8, 50, 62, 74, 6, 4, 88, 100, 58, 92, 96, 42, 38, 74, 16, 12

Page 29

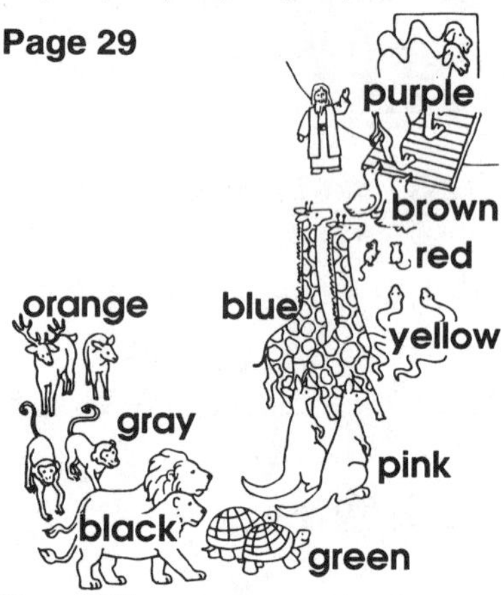

Page 30

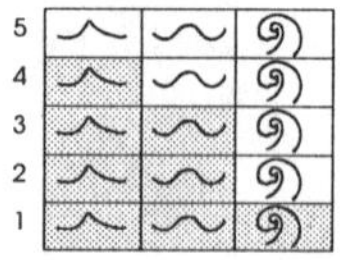

Page 31

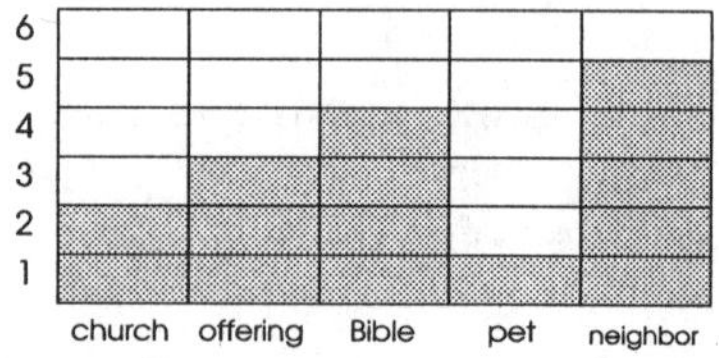

Page 32

taller: hippo, bear, cat; shorter: grasshopper, butterfly, cow

Page 33

Ark is 7 zebra counters tall.
Ark is 10 zebra counters wide.
Ark is 3 elephant counters tall.
Ark is 4 elephant counters wide.

Page 34

Noah is 12 raccoon counters tall. Noah's arm is 4 raccoon counters long. Noah's foot is 1 camel counter long. Noah's staff is 5 camel counters tall.

Page 35

hippo—1 in. tall, 2 in. wide
butterfly—1 in. tall, 1 in. wide
turtle—1 in. tall, 1 in. wide
elephant—2 in. tall, 2 in. wide
giraffe—3 in. tall, 1 in. wide
flamingo—2 in. tall, 1 in. wide

Page 36

8 cm, 9 cm, 5 cm, 3 cm, 2 cm

Page 37

Estimates will vary; actual 1 in., 6 in., 5 in., 12 cm, 8 cm

Page 38

3:00, 7:00, 10:00;
5:00, 12:00, 6:00

Page 39

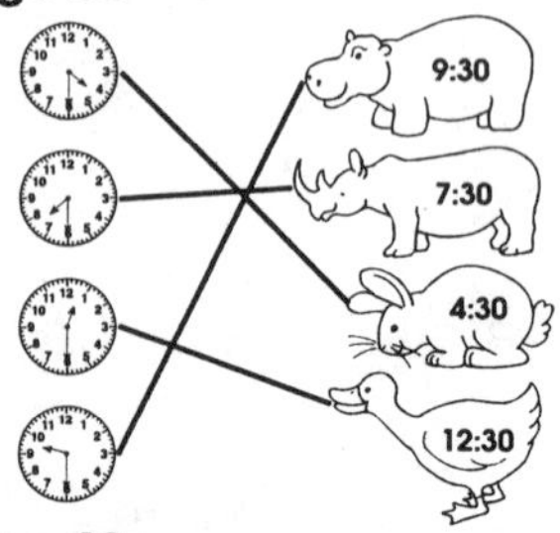

Page 40

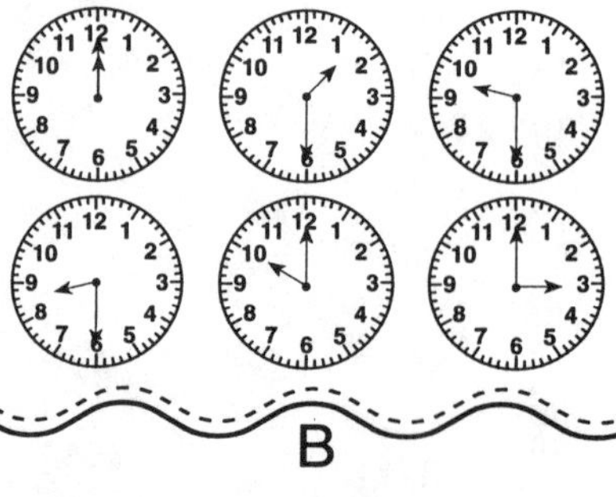

Page 41

Page 42

3/4, 2/3, 1/2, 1/3, 2/4,

Page 43

1/2, 2/4; 2/3, 3/6; 1/3, 3/4

Page 44

circle—9, rectangle— 11, square—10, triangle—17

Page 45

27¢, 18¢, 23¢, 34¢

Page 46

stripes of rainbow: red, orange, yellow, green, blue

Page 47

Monday; March 17th; March 25th; March 7th; March 27th

Page 48

1, 6, 2, 4, 7, 5, 3; Tuesday, Thursday, Friday

Page 49

A, 1—ark; C, 0—dove;
C, 2—Noah; A, 3—zebra;
B, 3—cloud; B, 1—alligator

Page 50

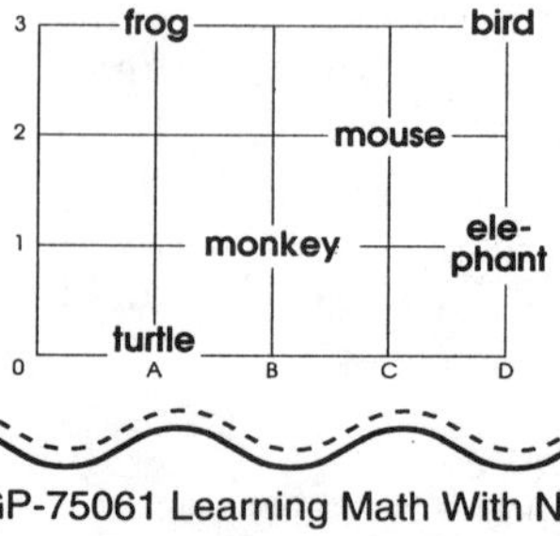

Using the Manipulatives

Below are suggestions of activities you can do using the manipulatives on pages 51-52.

Ark Animal Counters

Color and cut out the ark animal counters on page 51. Try these suggested activities:

1. Use the ark animal counters to practice addition and subtraction activities presented in this book.
2. Tell addition and subtraction stories using the animal counters.
3. Make patterns using the animal counters.
4. Group the animal counters by ones, twos, fives, and tens. Count how many ark animals in all.
5. Mix up the ark animal counters and put them in a stack. Pick up some of the counters. Make a graph to show how many of each were picked up, tell which fraction of the set the animals are, and identify of which animal there is the greatest amount.
6. Use the animal counters to practice the measuring activities presented in this book.

Measurement Aids

Color and cut out the inch ruler and centimeter ruler on page 52. Try these suggested activities:

1. Use the rulers to practice measurement activities presented in this book.
2. Measure items around the classroom or the home.
3. Create a picture using exactly measured inch and centimeter lines.

Clock

Cut out the clock face and hands on page 52. Use a brass fastener to assemble the clock. Try these suggested activities:

1. Use the clock to practice telling time on activities presented in this book.
2. Show favorite times of the day on the clock and say the time to an adult.

Faithful First-Grader

Congratulations!

You have learned all of your math skills!

Presented to ______________________
Name

on ______________
Date

Even Elephants

Noah even had room for elephants on the ark.

Color the spaces with even numbers gray. Color the spaces with odd numbers blue.

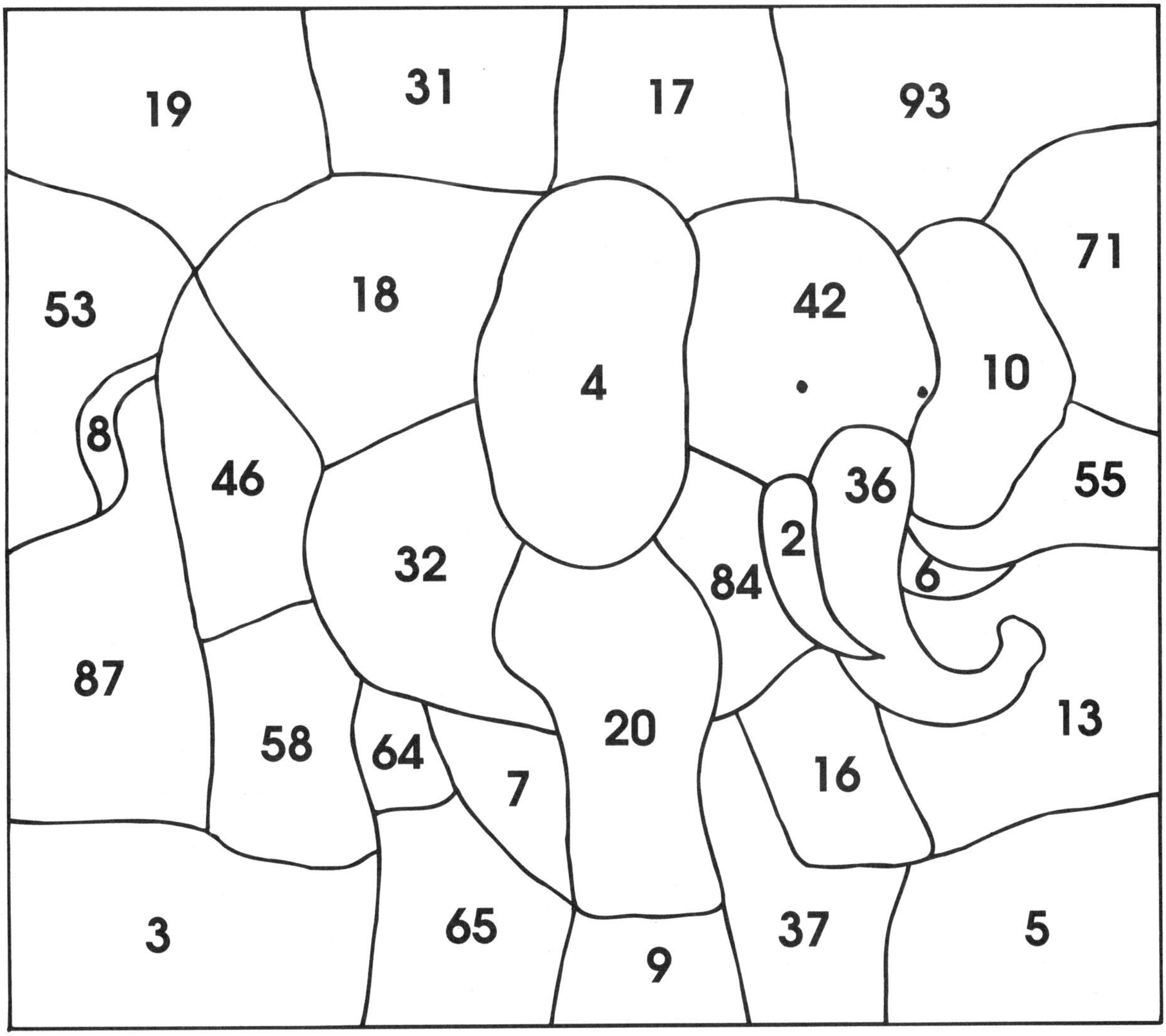

Odd Ostriches

The ostrich is the largest bird God created.

Color the spaces with odd numbers green. Color the spaces with even numbers yellow.

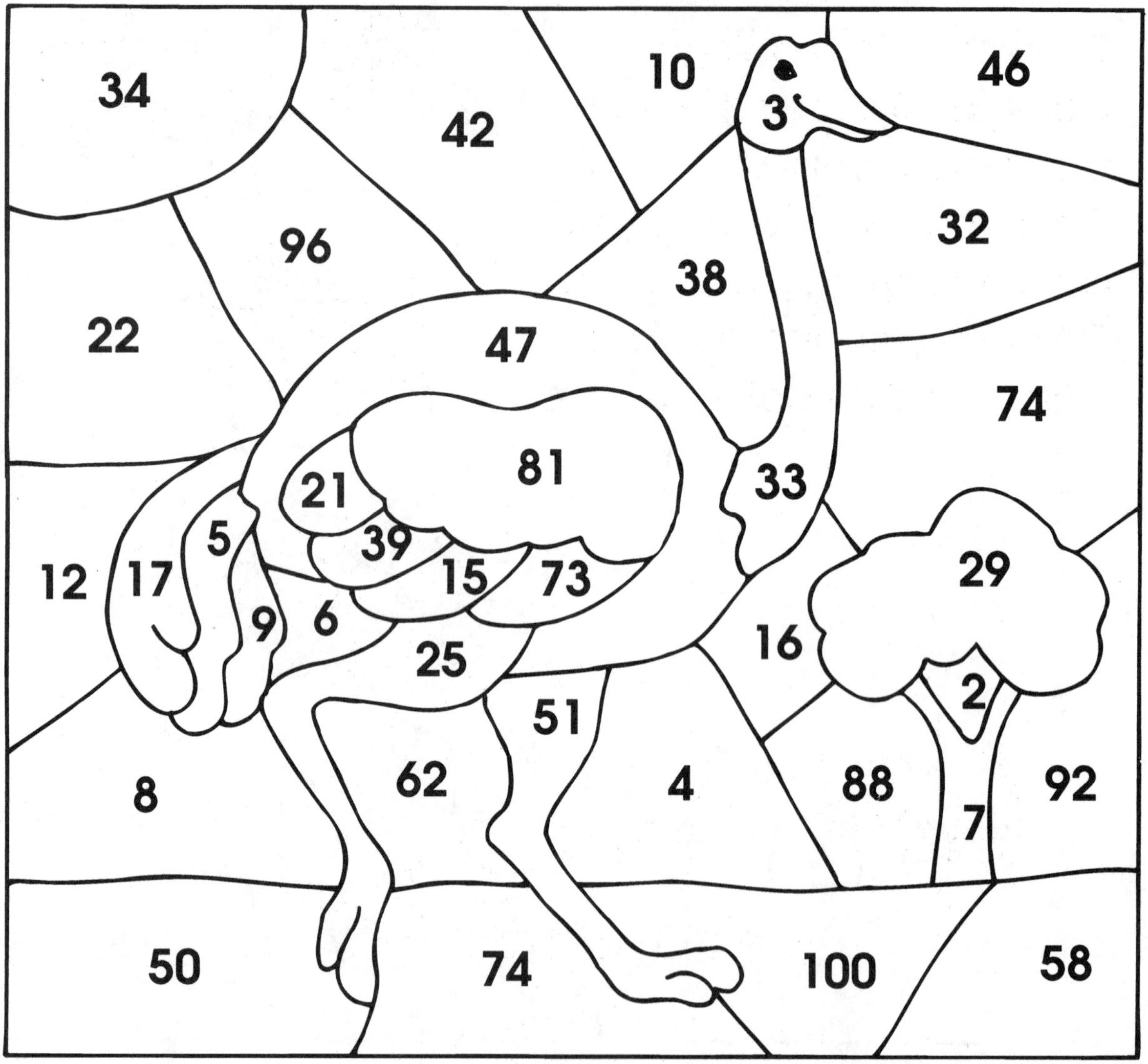

Animals Raced In

The animals entered the ark in pairs, two by two.

Color the fifth pair of animals blue.
Color the seventh pair green.
Color the third pair red.
Color the ninth pair gray.
Color the first pair purple.
Color the eighth pair black.
Color the fourth pair yellow.
Color the tenth pair orange.
Color the second pair brown.
Color the sixth pair pink.

Waves of Wonder

God kept his promise to Noah. He protected the ark from danger during the flood. The ark was not hurt by the waves of wonder!

Look at the waves around the ark. Color one picture on the graph for each wave of wonder you see.

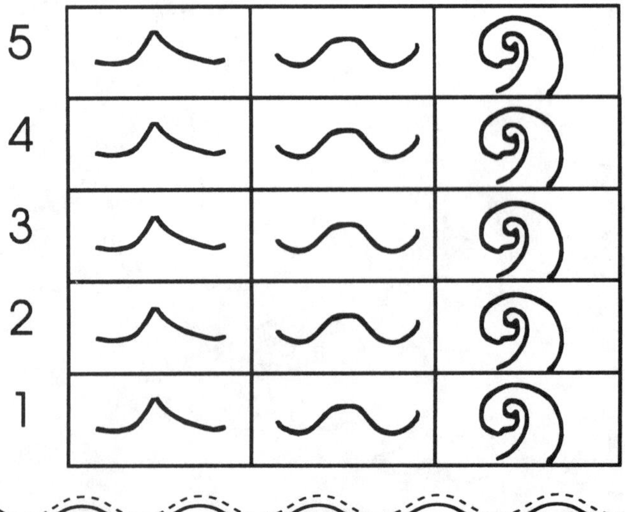

Keeping the Faith

Noah was a faithful man. We are called to be faithful to God, too. We show our faithfulness every day when we obey God.

Look at the pictures of the children. Color one box on the graph for each faithful child of God.

	church	offering	Bible	pet	neighbor
6					
5					
4					
3					
2					
1					

All Shapes and Sizes

God told Noah to save two of every animal. God created animals in lots of shapes and sizes. God loves all animals. He loves us, too!

Color the taller animal in each box.

Color the shorter animal in each box.

What a Big Ark!

God told Noah exactly how to make the ark. God told Noah how high, how wide, and how long it should be. Noah built it exactly that way.

Using the ark animal counters on page 51, measure the height and width of Noah's ark.

How many zebra counters tall is the ark? ______

How many zebra counters wide is the ark? ______

How many elephant counters tall is the ark? ______

How many elephant counters wide is the ark? ______

What a Faithful Man!

Noah was 600 years old when he entered the ark.

Using the animal counters on page 51, find the measurements below.

Noah is ________ raccoon counters tall.

Noah's arm is ________ raccoon counters long.

Noah's foot is ________ camel counters long.

Noah's staff is ________ camel counters tall.

How Big Were the Animals?

Noah brought every kind of creature that moves along the ground into the ark. They were all different sizes.

Using an inch ruler, measure the height and width of the animals.

_______ in. tall

_______ in. wide

_______ in. tall

_______ in. wide

_______ in. tall

_______ in. wide

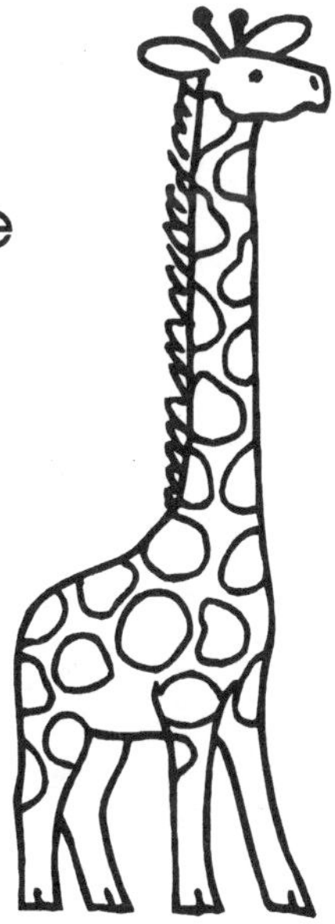

_______ in. tall

_______ in. wide

_______ in. tall

_______ in. wide

_______ in. tall

_______ in. wide

Great Waves

The waters made the ark rise high above the earth.

Using a centimeter ruler, measure the height of the waves around the ark.

Ark Estimation

God told Noah how to build the ark. It was to be 450 feet long, 75 feet wide, and 45 feet high.

Estimate the length of each line of the ark. Write your estimate in the box. Then find the actual measurement. Write it in the circle.

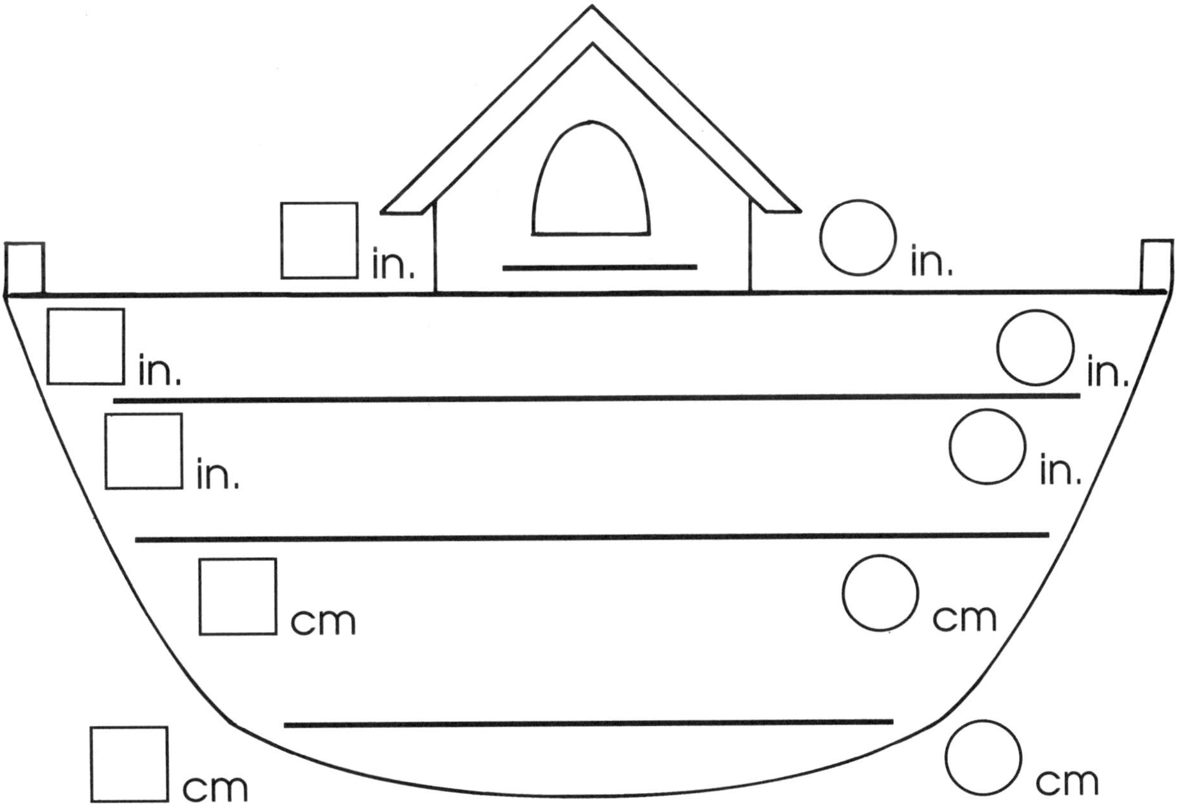

Time Went By

Noah was patient as time went by in the ark. He trusted God's plan and was faithful.

Write the time.

______ ______ ______

______ ______ ______

The Hours Passed

Sometimes we must be like Noah and wait patiently for God's plan.

Draw a line to match the times.

Writing time to the hour and half-hour

Feeding Time

Noah fed and cared for the animals in the ark every day. He was probably busy all day.

Draw the hands on the clocks.

12:00

1:30

9:30

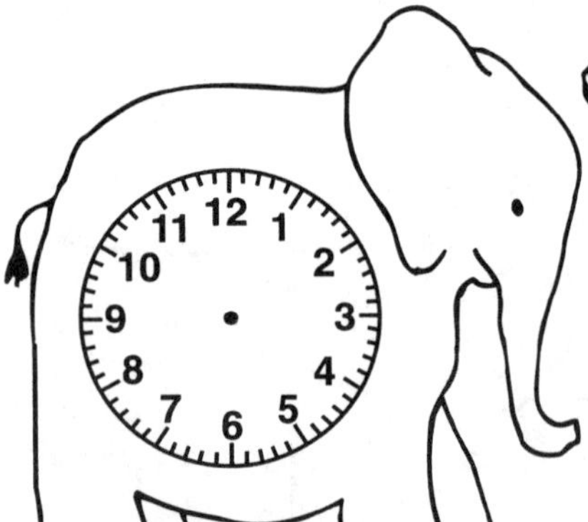

8:30

10:00

3:00

Noah Cared for Them Equally

Just as God cares for us and loves us all the same, Noah treated each animal equally.

Color the correct amount of parts for each fraction. Or, fill in the correct missing fraction.

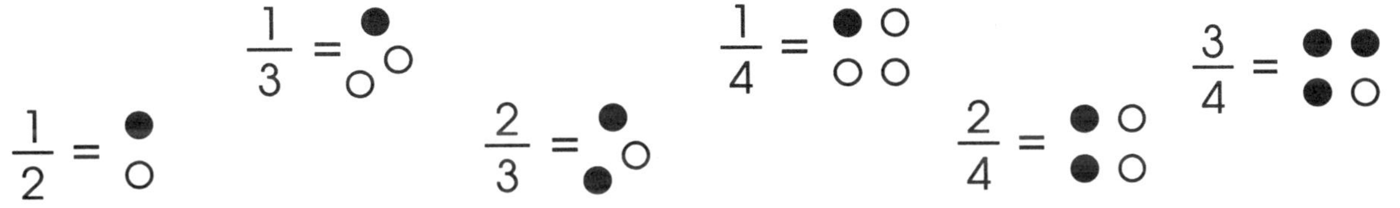

$\frac{1}{2}$ 	___ 
$\frac{1}{4}$ 	___ 
___ 	$\frac{1}{3}$ 

The Rain Stopped

God remembered Noah and the animals. God stopped the rain. The water slowly went down. Noah and his family must have been happy to see the sun.

Look at each sun. Write the fraction to show the shaded part.

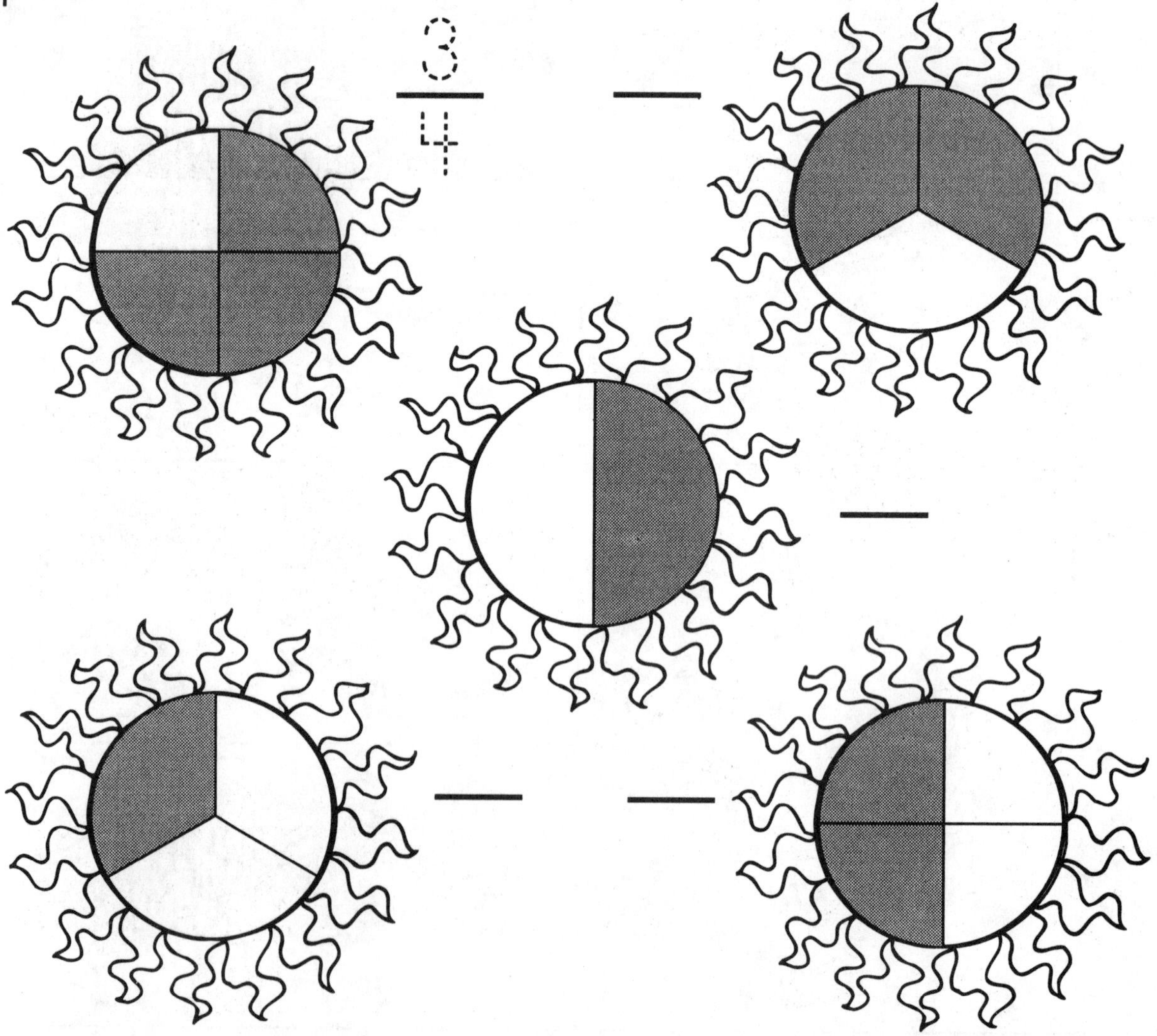

It's Time to Leave the Ark

After the rain stopped, Noah opened a window and sent out a dove. The dove returned to Noah with an olive leaf in its beak. That showed Noah that water was no longer covering the land.

Look at each olive branch. Write the fraction of the number of leaves shaded.

$\frac{1}{2}$ 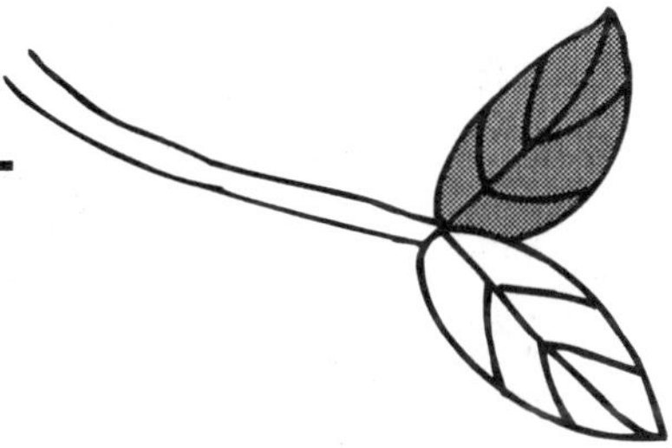

___ 

___ 

___ 

___ 

___ 

Ark Shapes

It took Noah 120 years to build the ark.

Find the shapes below.

Color and count the number of shapes.

red ◯ ____ green ▭ ____

blue □ ____ brown △ ____

God's Promises Are Priceless

God promised to never again destroy every living thing with a flood. God gave us the rainbow as a sign of that promise. Count the coins in each cloud. Write the amount.

Treasure God's Promises

God gives us many promises to treasure. Every time we see a rainbow, we can remember God's promise.

Count the money in each line. Use the key to color the rainbow.

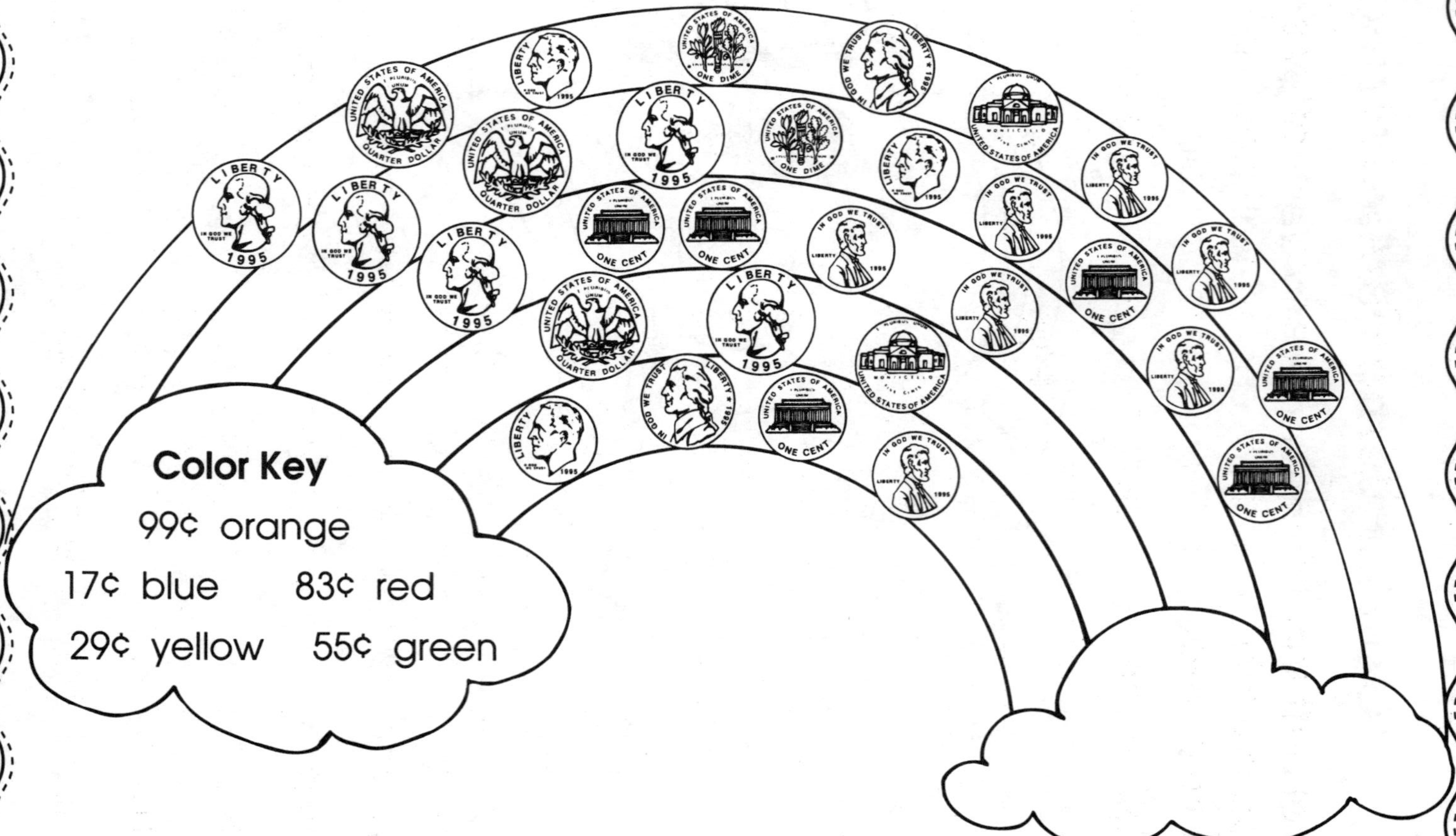

Time Gone By

Noah left the ark a little over a year after entering it. Man created a way to measure time. Twelve months make a year.

Look at the calendar. Answer the questions.

March						
Sunday	Monday	Tuesday	Wednesday	Thursday	Friday	Saturday
	1	2	3	4	5	6
7	8	9	10	11	12	13
14	15	16	17	18	19	20
21	22	23	24	25	26	27
28	29	30	31			

On what day does the month begin? ____________________

What is the date of the third Wednesday? _______________

What is the date two weeks after March 11? _____________

What is the date of the first Sunday? ____________________

What is the date of the last Saturday? ____________________

God Keeps the Promise

We need to count God's blessings every day and be thankful for God's promises. God is faithful to us, and we need to be faithful every day of the week. Seven days make a week.

Read the days of the week. Number them in order starting with Sunday.

_______ Sunday

_______ Friday

_______ Monday

_______ Wednesday

_______ Saturday

_______ Thursday

_______ Tuesday

Write the names of the missing days.

Sunday	Monday		Wednesday			Saturday

They Have Arrived

God also protected Noah and his family. Then God commanded the family to be fruitful, multiply, and fill the earth.

Look at the graph. Using coordinates, identify the object where the points meet.

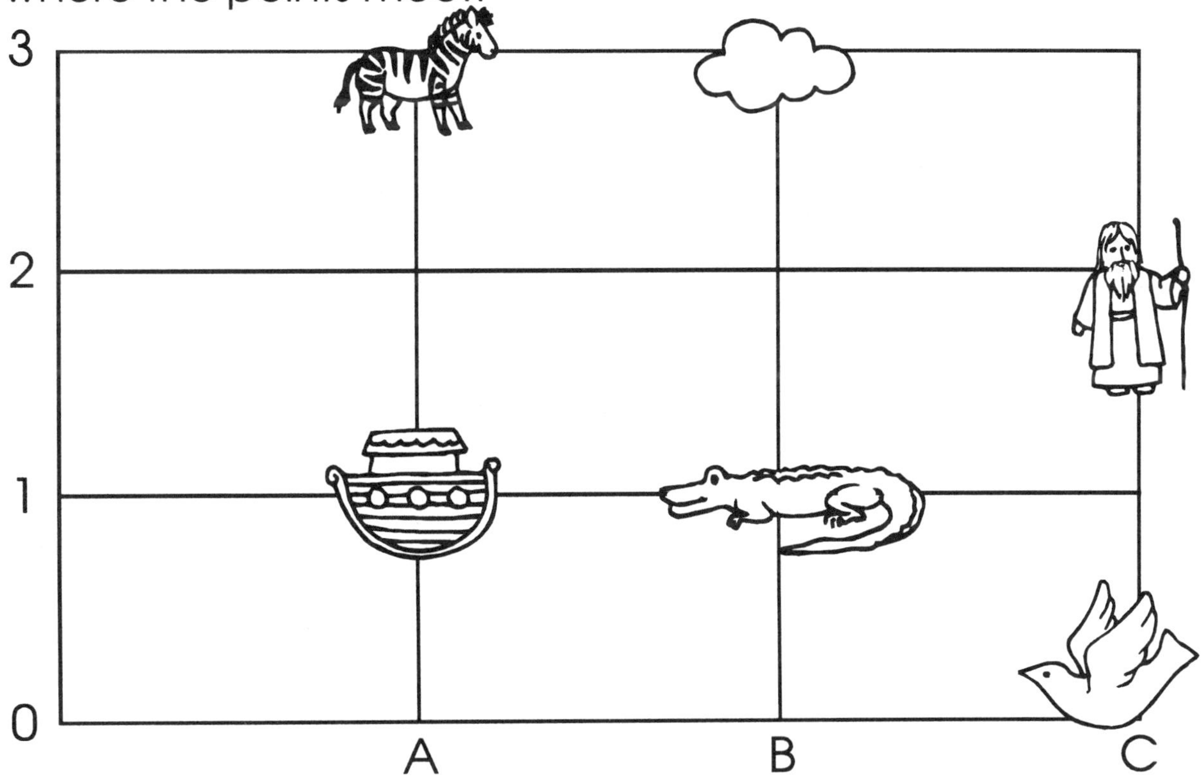

A, 1 ____________________

C, 0 ____________________

C, 2 ____________________

A, 3 ____________________

B, 3 ____________________

B, 1 ____________________

Back on Land

Imagine how happy the animals must have been to be back on land!

Use the coordinates to draw the animals on the grid.

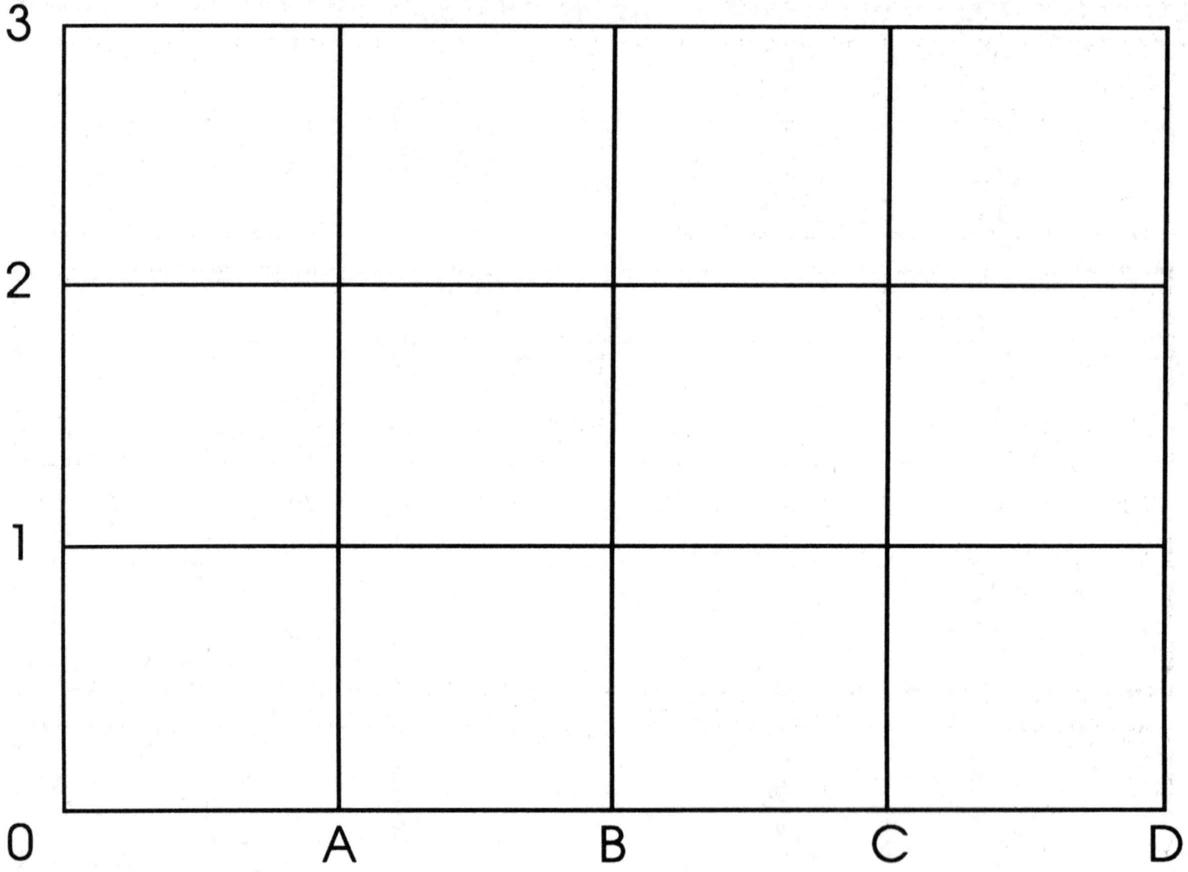

frog	A, 3	monkey	B, 1
elephant	D, 1	mouse	C, 2
turtle	A, 0	bird	D, 3

Ark Animal Counters

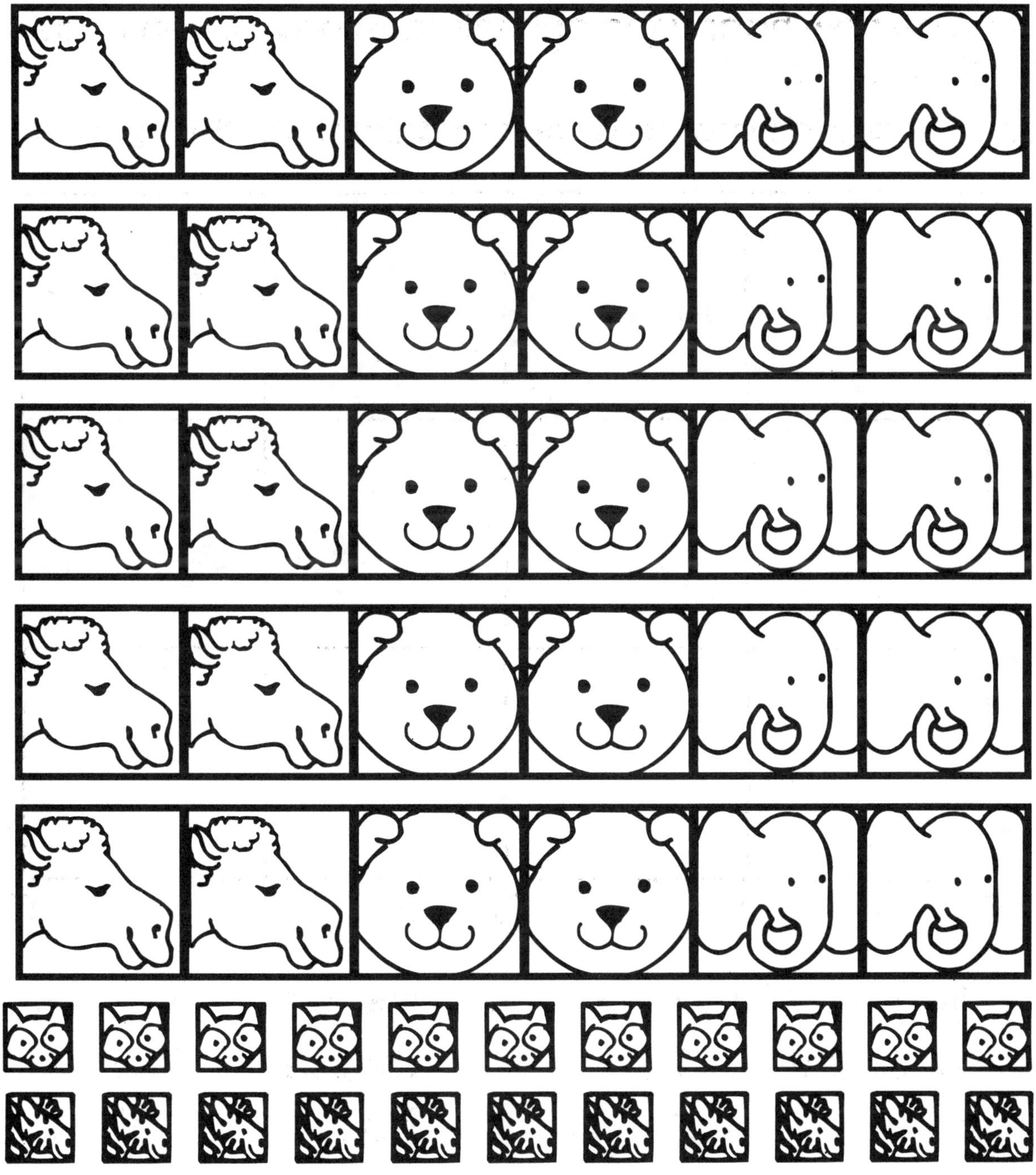

Measurement Aids

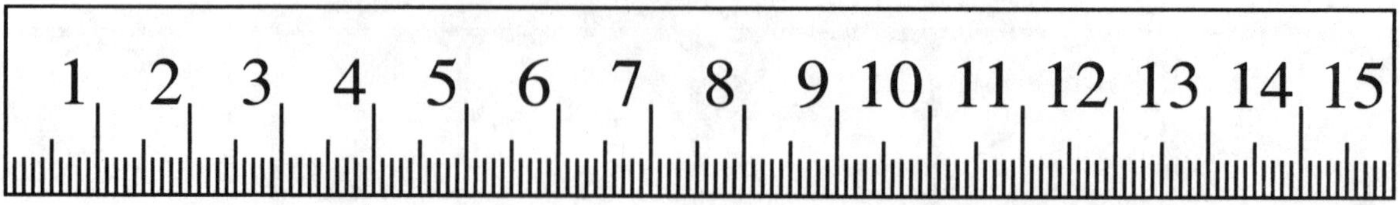

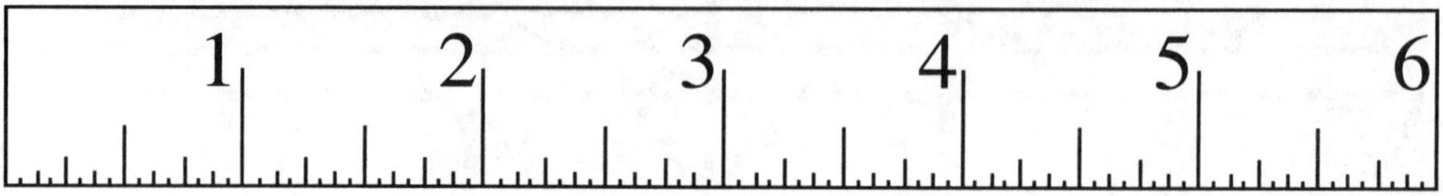

Use a brass fastener
to assemble clock.